Our Raspberry Jam

By David F. Marx
Illustrated by Paul Michalak

Children's Press®
A Division of Grolier Publishing
New York • London • Hong Kong • Sydney
Danbury, Connecticut

To my wife. Even though you are not a doctor,
I want to thank you for all of your patients during
the making of this story. Thanks Amy.
–P.M.

Reading Consultants
Linda Cornwell
Coordinator of School Quality and Professional Improvement
(Indiana State Teachers Association)

Katharine A. Kane
Education Consultant
(Retired, San Diego County Office of Education
and San Diego State University)

Visit Children's Press® on the Internet at:
http://publishing.grolier.com

Library of Congress Cataloging-in-Publication Data
Marx, David F.
    Our raspberry jam / by David F. Marx ; illustrated by Paul Michalak.
        p. cm.—(Rookie reader)
    Summary: A girl feasts on the wonderful raspberry jam that she and her family have made
and remembers that she loves it because they made it together.
    ISBN 0-516-22174-4 (lib. bdg.)   0-516-27151-2 (pbk.)
    [1. Jam—Fiction. 2. Raspberries—Fiction. 3. Cookery—Fiction.] I. Michalak, Paul,
ill. II. Title. III. Series.
PZ7.M36822 Ou 2000
[E]—dc21   99-088534

On just the right day
last September,
we went to the farm.

Mom said the raspberries
were perfect for picking.

So red and plump!

We picked pint after
pint of raspberries.

I ate a few along the way.

Dad paid a little extra
for the ones I ate.

At home, we washed them,
picked out leaves,

and got rid of bugs . . . ick!

Then, it was time to make our jam!

First, we mashed the raspberries
in our biggest pot.

Then, we cooked them
with water and sugar.

Our kitchen smelled like candy!

We poured the jam into jars

and closed the lids tight.

Mom put away most of the jars
to give as gifts.

But we saved a BIG jar just for us.

For a whole week, I ate that great jam at every meal.

Then, I was sick of raspberry jam.

23

When the holidays came,
we gave jam to everyone we knew!

But then today, a cold day
deep in February,

I found one more jar
in the back of the pantry.

I remember why
I love our raspberry jam.

I love it because we made it!

Word List (112 words)

a	deep	jam	our	so
after	every	jar	out	sugar
along	everyone	jars	paid	that
and	extra	just	pantry	the
as	farm	kitchen	perfect	them
at	February	knew	picked	then
ate	few	last	picking	tight
away	first	leaves	pint	time
back	for	lids	plump	to
because	found	like	pot	today
big	gave	little	poured	us
biggest	gifts	love	put	was
bugs	give	made	raspberries	washed
but	got	make	raspberry	water
came	great	mashed	red	way
candy	holidays	meal	remember	we
closed	home	Mom	rid	week
cold	I	more	right	went
cooked	ick	most	said	were
Dad	in	of	saved	when
day	into	on	September	whole
	it	one	sick	why
		ones	smelled	with

About the Author

David F. Marx is a children's author and editor who lives in the Chicago area. He is the author of several other books in the Rookie Reader and Rookie Read-About Geography series for Children's Press.

About the Illustrator

Paul Michalak and his wife live in central New York where Paul works as an illustrator.